TEXAS

A province of Mexico until 1836

The map locates places in the story. Important events at each place are given with dates.

WASHINGTON
ON-THE-BRAZOS

ALAMO

GONZALES

SAN
ANTONIO
DE BEXAR

GOLIAD

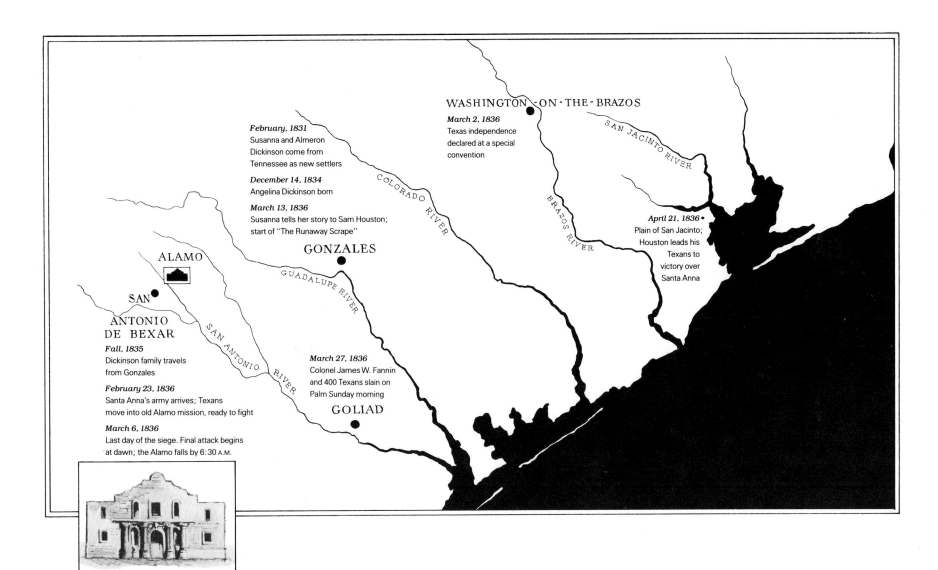

WASHINGTON - ON - THE - BRAZOS

March 2, 1836
Texas independence
declared at a special
convention

February, 1831
Susanna and Almeron
Dickinson come from
Tennessee as new settlers

December 14, 1834
Angelina Dickinson born

March 13, 1836
Susanna tells her story to Sam Houston;
start of "The Runaway Scrape"

April 21, 1836 •
Plain of San Jacinto;
Houston leads his
Texans to
victory over
Santa Anna

COLORADO RIVER

SAN JACINTO RIVER

BRAZOS RIVER

GONZALES

GUADALUPE RIVER

ALAMO

SAN
ANTONIO
DE BEXAR

Fall, 1835
Dickinson family travels
from Gonzales

February 23, 1836
Santa Anna's army arrives; Texans
move into old Alamo mission, ready to fight

March 6, 1836
Last day of the siege. Final attack begins
at dawn; the Alamo falls by 6:30 A.M.

SAN ANTONIO RIVER

March 27, 1836
Colonel James W. Fannin
and 400 Texans slain on
Palm Sunday morning

GOLIAD

*The familiar roof line of the chapel, known around the world
as the symbol of the Alamo, was not there at the time of the story.
It was added during repairs made in 1846. The year before, 1845,
the Republic of Texas became America's twenty-eighth state.*

Commandancy of the Alamo,
Bexar, Feby. 24th, 1896

To the People of Texas & all Americans in the world—

Fellow citizens & compatriots — I am besieged, by a thousand or more of the Mexicans under Santa Anna — I have sustained a continual Bombardment & cannonade for 24 hours & have not lost ... 'tis true that we are in great danger; a surrender at discretion, The greater therefore should our courage be. to the sword, if the fort is Shakespeare, *Henry V* answered the demand with a cannon shot, & our flag still waves proudly from the walls — I shall never surrender or retreat. Then, I call on you in the name of Liberty, of patriotism & everything dear to the American character, to come to our aid, with all dispatch — The enemy is receiving reinforcements daily & will no doubt increase to three or four thousand in four or five days. If this call is neglected, I am determined to sustain myself as long as possible & die like a soldier who never forgets what is due to his own honor & that of his country — Victory or Death.

Lt. Col. William B. Travis

HBJ

G U L L I V E R   B O O K S

H A R C O U R T   B R A C E   J O V A N O V I C H

San Diego   Austin   Orlando

SUSANNA
OF THE ALAMO
A True Story

Written by
JOHN JAKES

Designed and illustrated by
PAUL BACON

Dedicated to our wives.

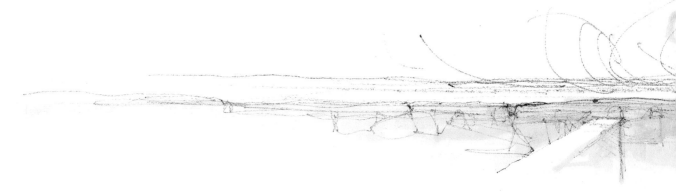

WITH THANKS...

The author and artist here pay tribute to those who helped us tell Susanna's story so that it is faithful to the historical record. (Gaps do exist; and some "facts" live on in different versions.)

Leo Zuniga of HBJ opened doors for us in San Antonio. There, Mrs. Edith May Johnson, Alamo committee chairman and director of the Daughters of the Republic of Texas, the group that oversees the historical site with care and devotion, shared valuable time and knowledge. So did Henry Guerra, chairman of the Bexar County Historical Society, a man of good humor and vast information. Mrs. June Barth of the Daughters of the Republic guided us through what remains of the original Alamo compound. Bernice Strong of the D. R. T. Library at the Alamo clarified several important points.

Additional help with gathering research material and comparing versions of the story from different sources came from the author's wife, Rachel Jakes. And along the way, we have enjoyed the friendship and support of Willa Tupper, our editor at Gulliver Books, and Rubin Pfeffer, editor-in-chief of HBJ trade books, who gave the two of us the happy opportunity to work together.

As noted, questions still exist about parts of the Alamo story. Legends have sprung up to improve on what might have happened, as legends have a way of doing. We have avoided the legends, no matter how attractive, and invented nothing except some of the dialogue. This book contains no fictional characters or events. Where a fact is debated by historians, we chose the most widely accepted version.

Finally, while acknowledging the generous help of those people named, we must add that they are in no way responsible for possible mistakes of fact or interpretation. That responsibility belongs to us.

—J. J. and P. B.

Library of Congress Cataloging-in-Publication Data
Jakes, John, 1932-
    Susanna of the Alamo.
    Summary: Relates the experiences of the Texas woman who, along with her baby, survived the 1836 massacre at the Alamo.
    1. Alamo (San Antonio, Tex.)—Siege, 1836—Juvenile literature.
2. Dickenson, Susanna—Juvenile literature. 3. Pioneers—Texas—Biography—Juvenile literature. 4. Women pioneers—Texas—Biography—Juvenile literature. 5. Texas—Biography—Juvenile literature. [1. Alamo (San Antonio, Tex.)—Siege, 1836. 2. Dickenson, Susanna.
3. Pioneers. 4. Texas—Biography] I. Bacon, Paul, 1923— . II. Title.

F390.J2 1986   976.4'03 [92]   85-27143

ISBN 0-15-332877-0   (Library: 10 different titles)
ISBN 0-15-332916-5   (Single title, 4 copies)
ISBN 0-15-332976-9   (Replacement single copy)

San Antonio de Bexar, in the Mexican province of Texas. February 23, 1836.

"Look there, Sue!" cried a young blacksmith named Almeron Dickinson. "I know that signal. The red flag means the Mexican soldiers will show no mercy. Their general, Santa Anna, wants to scare us."

The young woman standing beside him, his wife, Susanna, was already afraid. She feared for Almeron and for their daughter, Elizabeth Angelina, almost fifteen months old.

Earlier that day, General Santa Anna's army rode into the town of San Antonio. Many people left after learning that more soldiers were on the way. But the Dickinsons and more than 150 other Texans didn't run. They moved inside an old mission called the Alamo and turned it into a fort.

Susanna felt a sudden chill as she and Almeron stood together on the Alamo wall. Was it caused by the winter weather, or their danger?

"Won't Santa Anna talk with us?" she said to him. "Mexico used to be friendly to Americans. We were asked to come to Texas to fill up the land. Mexico wanted settlers."

"But then Santa Anna became President. He took away our rights," replied Almeron. "No use talking to a man like that—a dictator. All we can do is stand up for what we believe."

Susanna was only 22. She couldn't read or write, but she was a caring mother—a loving wife. She and Almeron had come to San Antonio last fall, from the village of Gonzales. Gonzales was their home after they moved to Texas from Tennessee in 1831.

Life had been good in Gonzales. Susanna and Almeron were young, strong, hopeful.

But now, as she gazed at the red flag, Susanna worried about the future. Were they going to lose everything in a fight for freedom?

ALMERON DICKINSON

The Texans defending the Alamo hoped to block the advance of Santa Anna's army and gain time for General Sam Houston, leader of the much smaller Texas army, to gather more men.

The stone and adobe buildings of the old mission were strong but partly in ruins. Once, Franciscan priests had lived there, and then some soldiers from Alamo de Parras in Mexico. Those soldiers were well liked by the local people, who nicknamed them *"los Alamos."* When the soldiers left, the name stuck to the place that had sheltered them.

Those in the Alamo with Susanna and Almeron also came from far places: Massachusetts. Pennsylvania. Tennessee. Europe. One had even served in Napoleon's army, years before.

There was former Congressman Davy Crockett of Tennessee, famous for tall stories and for killing ferocious bears that attacked him. He rode all the way from Tennessee to help. He brought 12 men,

DAVY CROCKETT

his fiddle, and a long rifle he called Betsy.

There was Jim Bowie, an adventurer who carried a big hunting knife later named after him. He was supposed to share command of the Alamo but he got sick, so the other commander took charge.

He was William B. Travis, a 26-year-old lawyer from Alabama. His past was mysterious. Some trouble over a woman. But he was a strong leader.

Not everyone in the Alamo was American. Some

JIM BOWIE

COLONEL TRAVIS

of the Texans were Mexican, like Gregorio Esparza, who brought his wife and four children. He didn't like Santa Anna either. But the thought of fighting his own brother saddened him.

"Maybe your brother isn't with Santa Anna's army," said Susanna, trying to comfort Esparza.

"Yes, he is. He's afraid of *El Presidente*. But we must not be afraid to fight to be free of Santa Anna's unjust laws. Texans should be treated fairly—just like any citizen of Mexico."

"*El Presidente* started this war," Almeron said. "Too many Americans have settled in Texas. He thinks we're too strong now."

No one showed that strength more than Almeron, Susanna thought as they spoke. He was a kindly man, with the powerful arms and hands a blacksmith needed. As a smithy and former soldier, he knew artillery. He was in charge of the cannon brought into the Alamo. The sight of him, so brave and tall, made Susanna love him more than ever.

★

Later that day, one of Santa Anna's officers came to demand surrender. Travis ordered the Alamo's 18-pound cannon to fire one round—a thundering *No*.

But the defenders were surrounded. A siege began.

Next day, Susanna's fear grew. Almeron told her that from the wall, he saw many more Mexican soldiers arriving. Then she heard cannon fire and rifle shots.

Before the day was over, Travis wrote a letter saying the defenders would never give up. *Victory or Death*, he wrote, just above his name.

On the fourth day, 32 men from Gonzales risked their lives to gallop into the mission. They all made it. Many were friends of the Dickinsons.

The weather was bitter cold now. Bowie was still sick with pneumonia, and Travis was writing more letters pleading for help. He sent them out at night with messengers who bravely dashed on horseback through showers of bullets. Most of all, Travis needed the 400 armed Texans waiting at Goliad under the command of Colonel James Fannin.

Outside, Santa Anna's men kept digging trenches, each new one nearer to the Alamo. Before long, soldiers and Texans were so close they could shout insults at each other.

The situation was desperate.

Even so, a few happy moments gleamed. Travis liked Susanna's pretty daughter. He gave little Angelina one of his treasures, a ring set with a shimmering cat's-eye stone. Travis's slave, Joe, smiled with approval.

Now and then Davy Crockett scraped out a tune on his fiddle. Davy's music was one of the few happy sounds left.

One of Travis's messengers, James Bonham, appeared suddenly after riding all the way back from Goliad, 95 miles. He brought bad news. Fannin was hesitating with his 400 men. Bonham returned rather than abandon his friends.

If Bonham can be so brave, Susanna thought, *I must too.*

Ten days passed.
Eleven.
Twelve . . .

Gunfire from both sides remained steady. Santa Anna's military bands played during the night, so the Texans lost sleep. The Mexican army kept growing . . . to two thousand, then three.

Eating a supper of fried beans with Susanna, Almeron, exhausted, shook his head. "Sometimes I wonder why we're holding out, Sue. Killing isn't right, or good. Those soldiers out there don't want to die any more than we do."

"I know," she said softly. "But maybe we want to be free more than they do."

Gazing at her with love, he reached out and squeezed her hand. And nodded.

★

Before dawn on Sunday, March 6, Santa Anna's armies were stirring. Dozing in an old damp blanket with Angelina in her arms, Susanna woke suddenly.

"What is that music?" she whispered.

Guns were crackling outside the chapel. Artillery matches glowed near the cannon on the walls. Susanna stared into the horrified face of her friend Señora Esparza.

"You know what the bugle call means, Señora. Please tell me."

"Santa Anna is tormenting us. It is the *deguello.* It means the same thing as the big red flag. Show no mercy. Kill everyone."

Sharp as knives, the bugle notes flew through the air. Susanna clutched her baby. She heard shouting, ladders thumping against the Alamo walls.

She rushed into the plaza as the first enemy rocket lit the paling sky. She saw Travis running toward the north wall, carrying a sword and shotgun. Before Crockett and others pushed Susanna back inside to safety, she heard Travis cry, *"The Mexicans are upon us—!"*

Susanna's heart beat fast. With the other women and children, she huddled in the sacristy, a small room off the chapel. Hers was the only American face. But all the faces shared a common look. It seemed to say:

We are frightened. But we stayed here to show what we're made of.

Now it's time.

In the sacristy, Susanna never saw the final brief battle, only heard it:

Booming cannon.
Shouts of attackers and defenders.
Cries of wounded and dying.
Almeron calling orders to his cannoneers . . .
Angelina fretted, clutching her mother's apron.
Susanna knew the Texans were losing.
Suddenly, powder-stained, Almeron was there.
"Great God, Sue, the Mexicans . . ."

All of Santa Anna's bands were playing the *deguello* together, so everyone could hear it above the gunfire.
". . . they're inside the north wall. Hear them?"
"Viva Santa Anna! Viva Santa Anna!"
"If they spare you, save our child."
And he was gone.
Forever.

Such a short battle. Nearly over by six-fifteen in the morning.

The women and children still huddled together, at the mercy of the soldiers, and chance. Señora Esparza cried out when she glimpsed her husband fall in the chapel. Susanna remembered the bugles. *No mercy,* they said. *No quarter.*

More and more soldiers swarmed through the chapel. *Almeron's gone,* Susanna thought. She hugged Angelina tighter.

Grief fell on her like hammer-blows. She too wanted to cry out. Instead, she prayed.

At half past six, the last defender was gone. The Alamo had fallen. The women and children were ordered to move to a smaller room, the baptistry. Susanna felt the end was near.

She would do her best to meet it calmly. If there was time, she would beg the enemy to spare Angelina's life.

A soldier entered. He noticed Susanna's white face at once. His bayonet rose to strike—

"Stop!" An officer strode in. "Is there a Señora Dickinson here?"

For a minute she couldn't understand how he would know. But of course Santa Anna would have heard from people in town about the women and children in the Alamo.

She raised her hand. "Yes."

"Don't stand there," the officer growled. "Bring your child and come with me if you want to save your life."

He dragged her out, stepping over the smashed-down chapel doors.

"Blessed Lord forgive them," Susanna whispered when she saw the plaza.

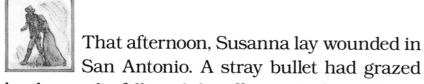

That afternoon, Susanna lay wounded in San Antonio. A stray bullet had grazed her leg as she followed the officer out of the Alamo. She had hardly felt it, searching for Almeron with tear-filled eyes.

She had seen Crockett where he fell at the palisade guns, his coonskin cap beside him. She had seen many familiar faces. But not Almeron's.

About 200 Mexicans died in the Alamo, and 188 Texans. She recalled only the fury of it. The senseless brutality of some of the enemy soldiers after the battle was won. The memories would never leave.

The doctor finished bandaging her wound. "It is light. You should be able to walk tomorrow. General Santa Anna will want to see you then, I am sure." His face showed dislike of his great commander.

"My husband—?" she began.

The doctor looked away. "I am sorry. They are all gone."

"But I must find Almeron! I must give him a decent burial. . . ."

"You must rest." He glanced at Angelina, his voice low. "Burial is impossible."

"Why?"

No answer.

Susanna suspected something horrible then. *"Tell me!"*

Ashamed, the doctor pointed to the smoke blowing past the window. "On the orders of the General, they are . . . burning all the dead. Except for a few of Mexican ancestry. A man named Esparza—he will receive burial. The rest—"

The doctor could barely speak. "It is the greatest shame for a fallen soldier, you see. Not to be buried."

A strange kind of lump, harder and hotter than sorrow could ever bring, filled Susanna's throat for a moment.

"I want to meet this great general of yours."

"You will. But I advise you not to be so eager."

Susanna couldn't sleep that night. She couldn't stop crying either. She tried to cry softly so as not to wake Angelina.

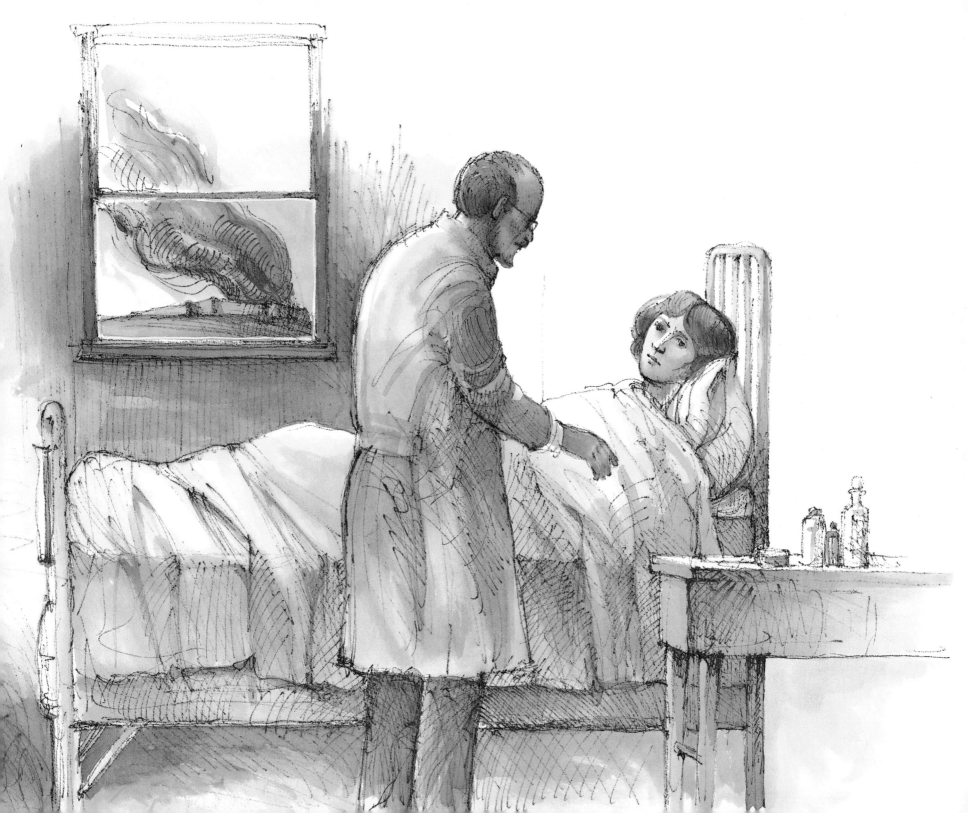

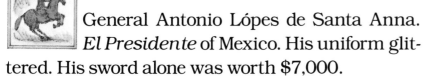 General Antonio Lópes de Santa Anna. *El Presidente* of Mexico. His uniform glittered. His sword alone was worth $7,000.

Puffed up with victory, he summoned the survivors of the Alamo before him, all but Susanna, who was not yet well enough. To each—the wives and sweethearts of the Texans who fell, and Travis's black servant, Joe—he gave $2 and a blanket.

Like an actor, he strode around the room, waving his arms dramatically and boasting in a loud voice:

"I do not make war upon women and children! Neither do I make war on slaves. Humane rules govern my army!"

When Susanna was able to meet Santa Anna, he repeated his boastful speech, then offered a blanket and money.

"Thank you, I don't want them," she said.

Santa Anna frowned. His well-known charm and exaggerated kindness were not working with this woman. What else could he try?

His eye fell on Angelina. He beamed.

"Señora Dickinson, please bring your daughter here to me."

Susanna didn't want the cruel man to touch Angelina. But with soldiers on guard around the room, she decided she had better obey.

"What a beautiful child," the general purred, holding Angelina.

Susanna said nothing.

"The rebellion will fail, you know. Your charming little girl should not stay in Texas. She's much too pretty to waste her life in a place as troubled as this. Let me send her to Mexico City. See to her education. The capital has fine schools. I will pay for everything personally."

"No, General. Texas is Angelina's home. And mine."

He didn't like that answer. His great show of humanity was failing.

"I will send you with her. You'll be far more comfortable—"

Her grief and anger were so great, she couldn't speak. She shook her head.

"Then I will send you somewhere else. A free woman."

"I said I don't want a blanket, or your—"

"Be still! You will go tell your Texan rebels what happened to those who dared to oppose me. You will describe it exactly. You will say it will happen to them if they continue their stupid little war."

He reached for pen and paper. "You will also carry a letter to all Texans willing to obey Mexican law once again."

He pointed to Colonel Almonte's orderly standing close by. "Ben will go with you to make sure you do as I command. You will go when your wound is better. You are a fool to refuse my generous offer, Señora. All of you Texans are fools, because it is impossible to fight me and win. Tell them Santa Anna is coming."

Susanna just stared at him.

Susanna rode toward Gonzales. She hoped to find General Sam Houston and his men there. Ben led the way.

On the road they met Travis's slave, Joe. Susanna asked him about Colonel Travis. "Gone," Joe said sadly. After the battle, Santa Anna walked through the Alamo himself, to be sure the leaders had not escaped. Crockett. Bowie. Travis . . .

"And Almeron?"

"He fell beside his guns on the chapel wall," Joe told her.

Almeron. Almeron . . .

She loved him so much.

★

The rain was cold and stinging, like defeat. Susanna carried Angelina and the letter Santa Anna wrote to the Texans. A letter full of false friendliness. She knew that her story was the real message he was sending:

Give up. It's hopeless. Listen to what happened. Keep fighting and the same will happen to you.

Ben heard her soft crying. "Miz Dickinson? You want to stop and rest?"

She did, but she remembered all the brave men. She was the only witness to the courage of those who died for both sides, all victims of Santa Anna's cruelty.

She was determined to find General Houston and deliver the message.

She owed it to Almeron. To all the fallen. She would deliver the message in a way that would make Santa Anna sorry he ever sent it.

"Miz Dickinson—?"

"No, Ben. We must go on."

The messengers continued through the storm.

Citizens!
It became necessary to check and chastise
a parcel of audacious adventurers...
Bexarians!
Return to your homes and dedicate
yourselves to your domestic duties...
Inhabitants of Texas!
The good among you will have nothing to fear
~ Antonio López de Santa Anna ~

Two of Houston's scouts, seeking news from San Antonio, found the travelers on the road. The scouts took Susanna and the others back to Gonzales, arriving after nightfall on March 13.

Yes, the scouts said, General Houston was in Gonzales. But Susanna wasn't able to speak with him right away. Friends and neighbors surrounded her, asking about loved ones.

Susanna gathered her courage. What she had to tell them almost broke her heart:

"Only women and children got out of the mission."

"You mean all of the men died?" a wife of one of the Alamo soldiers exclaimed.

"Yes, all but Joe and the ones Colonel Travis sent for help."

Sobbing began then. Outcries of grief. The townspeople pressed closer, calling out family names.

"I told you. There isn't a man left. My Almeron died too. Santa Anna butchered them. He's marching this way right now, probably with at least two thousand soldiers."

Cries of fright mingled with wails of sorrow. The voices grew louder. Clutching Angelina, Susanna

General Sam Houston. Born 1793. A man with a hot temper. He could barely control it when Susanna gave him the letter from *El Presidente,* then told the story of the Alamo's last thirteen days. By the end, he was trembling with wrath.

"Did Santa Anna bury the men honorably, Mrs. Dickinson?"

"He burned them."

Houston's eyes were cold as a pond during a winter freeze. He called Santa Anna some names. Luckily Angelina wasn't old enough to understand.

heard them echo in her head. She would hear them as long as she lived.

Suddenly, a big man appeared and strode to her side. He tried to speak gently, but couldn't hide his rage.

"I know this is hard for you, Mrs. Dickinson. But I must hear the whole story. Every word. Are you strong enough—?"

She thought of Santa Anna. She remembered why she struggled so hard to make the long journey. She overcame her sadness and held Angelina close as she answered Sam Houston.

"Yes, sir. I am."

GENERAL
SAM
HOUSTON

Touching Susanna's hand, Houston said, "You're a brave woman. Now we must make plans. You said Santa Anna is marching this way. Every citizen must head east while we gather more men for the army. The supplies and food we can't take, we'll burn. I want nothing left for him or his troops. Not even Gonzales itself."

Destroy their own homes and retreat? Susanna couldn't believe it.

"You're going to forget those men at the Alamo, General?"

"Never."

Worn out, full of sorrow, she found it hard to believe him. She had told the story vividly—and he was ordering everyone to run.

What a sad end to the struggle. A very important struggle, she realized as Houston kept on talking, telling her some things she hadn't heard yet: While Santa Anna surrounded the Alamo, other men were meeting at Washington-on-the-Brazos and they declared independence from Mexico on March 2. Almeron and the rest had died for the new Republic of Texas and didn't even know it.

So had Colonel Fannin and his 400. On March 20, Mexican troops caught them near Goliad and forced them to surrender. They were held prisoner in town for a week, then taken to some woods on Palm Sunday morning and shot to death, every last one.

They all died for the new Republic.

But the Republic of Texas was already blowing to pieces, like leaves torn from a tree in the wind.

★

That very night, people in Gonzales packed up and fled eastward. Susanna and Angelina left with them. Before sunrise, Gonzales was burning—put to the torch on Houston's order.

Soon it seemed as if every settler in Texas was heading east. "The Runaway Scrape," people called it afterward.

Susanna didn't see Houston again. She lived with her memories.

Travis giving Angelina his cat's-eye ring.

Almeron saying goodbye in the chapel.

Santa Anna strutting.

The sad ride to Gonzales, then facing all the townsfolk. Telling of their loved ones' bravery— only to have Houston order everyone to *run!*

Awake or asleep, she was haunted by the memories. Often she said to herself, "I failed you, Almeron. I failed all of you."

Then, about a month and a half after the fall of the Alamo — late April — Susanna heard some news. Exciting news of what Sam Houston did at a place called San Jacinto.

"Oh, it must have been glorious," said the man who told her the story. He continued:

"After old Sam Houston left Gonzales, he kept running ahead of Santa Anna, like a fox chased by a hound dog. But foxy Sam did it on purpose. He hoped he could pull Santa Anna away from the main part of his army. He got lucky. He did it.

"Just last week, it was. April 21. Right by Buffalo Bayou and the San Jacinto River.

"Around the middle of the afternoon, old Sam saw an eagle in the sky. He took it as a good sign and decided to attack right away. He said to our boys, 'Victory is certain. Trust in God and fear not.'

"Sam and his men caught Santa Anna napping. I mean, Santa Anna really was taking a nap under a big oak tree in his camp when Sam's two little cannon opened up and our boys charged."

Amazed and thrilled, Susanna listened intently to every word.

Although badly outnumbered, Houston pushed through meadow grass tall as a man, then up a hill to a barricade the Mexicans had built when they set up camp. Storming the hill, the Texans shouted a rallying cry. A bullet pierced Houston's right boot, but he kept fighting. The battle lasted only eighteen minutes.

"The poor Mexican soldiers thought they'd get the same cruel treatment our men got in San Antonio. They were scared and I don't blame 'em. They ran around, throwing guns away and hollering, '*Me no Alamo—me no Alamo.*'"

Maybe Susanna should have smiled. But she couldn't. She had looked closely at the face of war. No person with any sense or feeling could do that and smile.

"Texas is really free now," the storyteller concluded. "Santa Anna got whipped for sure. Only trouble was, soon as the battle started, he jumped on a horse and left his men behind."

Susanna clenched her fist. "He got away?"

"Sure did, the slippery snake." The storyteller grinned. "Till next day, anyhow.

"Then, our boys found this ordinary-looking fellow hiding in some tall grass. They dragged him to General Houston. This fellow kept saying he was just an army private who escaped and stole some clothes from a slave cabin. Just a plain old private.

"The trick might have worked, but the other prisoners saw him and started yelling."

"Yelling what?" asked Susanna.

The storyteller laughed. *"El Presidente. EL PRESIDENTE!"*

"So he's caught?"

"Yes indeed. And old Sam made him write an order pulling every last Mexican soldier out of Texas."

Susanna clapped her hands. Her eyes filled with joyful tears. "I wish I could have been there. Even for a minute—"

"Oh, but you were. General Houston didn't forget one single word of the story you told. Just before the battle he reminded our boys not to forget, either.

"It stiffened up their backbones. They shouted like wild men when they charged at San Jacinto. Oh, you were there, all right."

"What did they shout?"

"Why—'*Remember Goliad.*' But mostly, '*Remember the Alamo . . .*'"

REMEMBER THE ALAMO

Would they have won if I hadn't gone to Gonzales? Susanna sometimes thought with a small, quiet pride as the years passed.

She remarried, and never spoke of the Alamo again until late in her life. Angelina grew up to bear a strong resemblance to her mother.

Susanna lived until 1883. Some forgot her name. No one forgot her story.

TEXAS

A province of Mexico until 1836

The map locates places in the story. Important events at each place are given with dates.

WASHINGTON
ON-THE-BRAZOS

ALAMO

GONZALES

SAN
ANTONIO
DE BEXAR

GOLIAD

WASHINGTON · ON · THE · BRAZOS

March 2, 1836
Texas independence
declared at a special
convention

February, 1831
Susanna and Almeron
Dickinson come from
Tennessee as new settlers

December 14, 1834
Angelina Dickinson born

March 13, 1836
Susanna tells her story to Sam Houston;
start of "The Runaway Scrape"

SAN JACINTO RIVER

COLORADO RIVER

BRAZOS RIVER

April 21, 1836 •
Plain of San Jacinto;
Houston leads his
Texans to
victory over
Santa Anna

ALAMO

GONZALES

GUADALUPE RIVER

SAN
ANTONIO
DE BEXAR

SAN ANTONIO RIVER

Fall, 1835
Dickinson family travels
from Gonzales

February 23, 1836
Santa Anna's army arrives; Texans
move into old Alamo mission, ready to fight

March 6, 1836
Last day of the siege. Final attack begins
at dawn; the Alamo falls by 6:30 A.M.

March 27, 1836
Colonel James W. Fannin
and 400 Texans slain on
Palm Sunday morning

GOLIAD

*The familiar roof line of the chapel, known around the world
as the symbol of the Alamo, was not there at the time of the story.
It was added during repairs made in 1846. The year before, 1845,
the Republic of Texas became America's twenty-eighth state.*

0
1
D 2
E 3
F 4
G 5
H 6
I 7
J 8